I0765106
Belonging to :

FAMILY
Coloring Funny

FAMILY
Coloring Funny

FAMILY
Coloring Funny

FAMILY
Coloring Funny

FAMILY
Coloring Funny

FAMILY
Coloring Funny

FAMILY
Coloring Funny

FAMILY
Coloring Funny

FAMILY
Coloring Funny

FAMILY
Coloring Funny

FAMILY
Coloring Funny

FAMILY
Coloring Funny

FAMILY
Coloring Funny

FAMILY
Coloring Funny

FAMILY
Coloring Funny

FAMILY
Coloring Funny

FAMILY
Coloring Funny

FAMILY
Coloring Funny

FAMILY
Coloring Funny

FAMILY
Coloring Funny

FAMILY
Coloring Funny

FAMILY
Coloring Funny

FAMILY
Coloring Funny

FAMILY
Coloring Funny

FAMILY
Coloring Funny

FAMILY
Coloring Funny

FAMILY
Coloring Funny

FAMILY
Coloring Funny

FAMILY
Coloring Funny

FAMILY
Coloring Funny

FAMILY
Coloring Funny

FAMILY
Coloring Funny

FAMILY
Coloring Funny

FAMILY
Coloring Funny

FAMILY
Coloring Funny

FAMILY
Coloring Funny

FAMILY
Coloring Funny

FAMILY
Coloring Funny

FAMILY
Coloring Funny

FAMILY
Coloring Funny

FAMILY
Coloring Funny

FAMILY
Coloring Funny

FAMILY
Coloring Funny

FAMILY
Coloring Funny

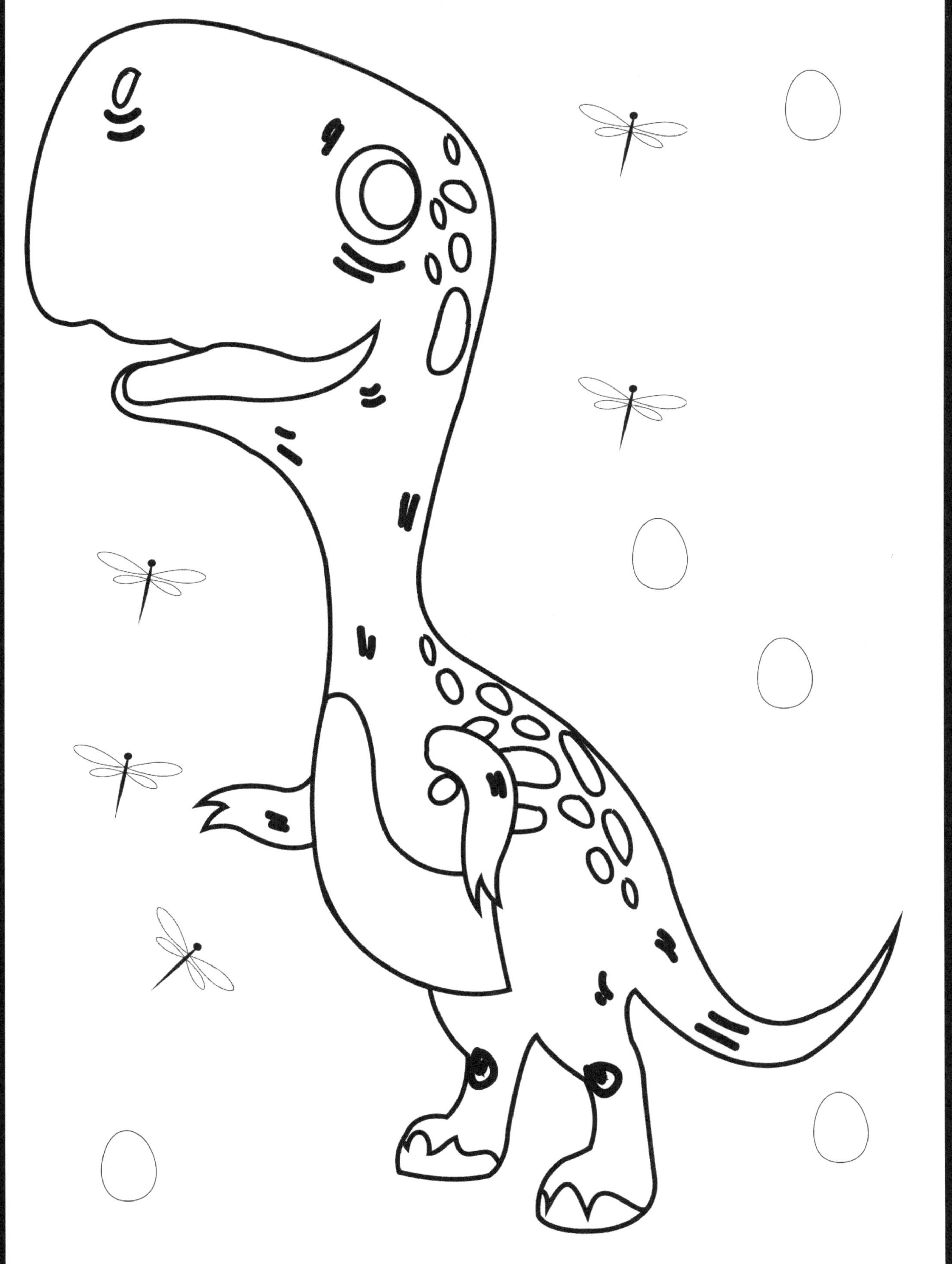

FAMILY
Coloring Funny

FAMILY
Coloring Funny

FAMILY
Coloring Funny

FAMILY
Coloring Funny

FAMILY

Coloring Funny